CW01465560

Kelterselber – Winemaking Made Easy:

Step-By-Step Guide for Hobby Winemakers

Dipl. -Ing. (FH) Tobias Gehring

Copyright © 2023 Tobias Gehring

All rights reserved.

ISBN: 9798867008420

Dedication

For Monja,

My irreplaceable life partner, who supports me uncon-
ditionally in all my undertakings. Your love and support
is a precious gift for me, and I am grateful for it from the
bottom of my heart.

With love and gratitude,

Tobias Gehring

Foreword

Dear readers,

Welcome to "Kelterselber – Winemaking Made Easy: Step-By-Step Guide for Hobby Winemakers".

This book shares my passion for winemaking. It is aimed at beginners, providing compact knowledge and complementing it with external sources. From the basics of fermentation to the selection of yeast and nutrients, I will guide you all the way to a delectable wine.

To access the useful Excel tool, send an email to:

kelterselber@yahoo.com

Dive into the fascinating world of winemaking and let your creativity run wild.

Cheers and happy reading! 🏆

Yours, Tobias Gehring, Graduate Engineer

TABLE OF CONTENTS

1. Basics – the key to success

Avoiding metal

The selection of the right materials is extremely important when it comes to winemaking. Metals, in particular, can cause undesirable effects by interacting with the acids present in the wine. Here are some recommendations that beginners should take into account:

- No zinc: The use of zinc in wine making should be strictly avoided. The fruit acid in wine can dissolve zinc and form toxic zinc salts that pose a serious health hazard to humans. Therefore, zinc objects should never come into contact with the wine.
- No brass: It is also advisable to avoid using brass utensils. Although the risk of direct poisoning is lower than with zinc, chemical reactions between brass and the acids in the wine can lead to a bitter taste and negatively affect the quality of the final product.
- Stainless steel: A recommendable and safe material for wine production is stainless steel. It is unreactive and does not affect the taste of the wine. Stainless steel utensils are therefore an excellent choice for beginners for making high-quality wine.
- Lacquered equipment: Equipment coated with acid-resistant lacquers can also be used in winemaking.

However, it is essential that these finishes are not damaged, otherwise the wine may react with the material underneath.

- Aluminium vessels: Although aluminium vessels may be acceptable for short periods of time, they should not be used for long periods of time in winemaking. The chemical reactivity of aluminium can cause undesirable changes in the taste and colour of the wine.

Selecting the fruit

The quality of the fruit used is a crucial factor in winemaking.

- Use ripe, healthy fruit: Only ripe and healthy fruit should be used for winemaking. Ripe fruits contain the optimal sugar content and the necessary aromatic substances essential for a high-quality wine.
- No rotten fruit: Rotten fruit can spoil the entire wine. Any rotten fruit should therefore be discarded to ensure the quality and taste of the final product.
- Cutting out rotten spots: If a piece of fruit is rotten in only a small area, that area can be carefully cut out so that the remaining healthy fruit can be used to make wine.

Keep light and air out

Preserving the wine's quality and aromas requires protection from light and air during the production process. Here are some important aspects that should be taken into account:

- Avoid oxygen: Oxygen can cause undesirable oxidation of valuable components in wine, negatively affecting aromas and flavours. It is therefore advisable to keep contact with air as low as possible during winemaking.
- Keep microorganisms away: Air can contain microorganisms, such as bacteria and yeast spores, which can have a detrimental effect on the final result. Careful hygiene and the use of clean equipment are therefore essential to prevent contamination of the wine.
- Keep away from sunlight: UV radiation from sunlight can also have negative effects on wine. Wine should therefore be protected from direct sunlight and stored in a dark room to preserve quality and aromas.

Cleanliness and rapidity

Cleanliness throughout the winemaking process is essential to prevent contamination by harmful microorganisms. Here are some important aspects:

- Freshly picked fruit: The use of freshly picked fruit is essential to preserve the quality of the wine and prevent premature fermentation.
- Immediate processing: Fruit should be processed as soon as possible after harvest to maintain its freshness and quality.
- Cleanliness when working: A hygienic working environment is essential to prevent the entry of harmful microorganisms.

2. What is needed to make wine?

As a budding winemaker, it is important to know the equipment needed:

Pure culture yeast

Pure culture yeast is essential in winemaking. These specially bred yeast strains enable precise and controlled fermentation. This allows winemakers to better monitor the entire fermentation process and develop the desired aromas and characteristics of the wine. Pure culture yeast offers reliable consistency in wine production and minimizes the risk of undesirable microbiological influences. The use of pure cultured yeast ensures efficient conversion of sugars into alcohol, which helps to improve the quality and taste of wine. Each yeast strain makes its own unique contribution to the complexity and nuance of the wine. Pure culture yeast allows winemakers to express their creative abilities and produce precise wines that meet the individual preferences of consumers. It is a tool to explore the rich diversity of wines and bring out the unique character of different grape varieties.

Sulphur sticks or potassium sulphite

Sulphur sticks or potassium sulphite have an important role to play in the preservation of wine. The targeted use of sulphur slows down the oxidation of the wine and at the same time kills unwanted microorganisms. This measure helps to preserve the freshness and quality of the wine over time. Nevertheless, it is essential to carefully control the dosage of sulphur. Excessive addition could negatively affect the taste and aroma of the wine.

Hose and fermentation tube

A hose is needed to transfer the wine from one fermentation container to another (decanting). The fermentation tube is used to remove excess carbon dioxide from the container during fermentation and at the same time to prevent air or harmful microorganisms from entering.

Fruits

The foundation for every wine is ripe, healthy fruit. Depending on the type of wine, different fruits are used, including apples, pears, cherries, strawberries, raspberries, grapes and other berries. The quality and ripeness of the fruit have a significant influence on the taste and aromas of the wine.

Nutrient salts for yeast

Nutrient salts are added to the yeast during fermentation to ensure efficient and complete fermentation. These salts promote the growth and vitality of the yeasts.

Sugar

Sugar is an important ingredient that starts the fermentation process. In most cases, sugar is added as a starter to stimulate fermentation and increase the alcohol content in the wine. The right amount of sugar is important for the desired alcohol content and the subsequent sweetness of the wine.

Glass marbles

Glass marbles are a clever and practical solution often used in winemaking to fill the fermentation vessel to the brim. These are small, glass balls from children's games, but also find a valuable use in wine production. The concept of bunging is important to optimally support the fermentation process of the wine. During the fermentation process, carbon dioxide is released, which collects in the fermentation vessel and could push the resulting wine upwards. This would create an air-filled space in the fermentation vessel, which could lead to unwanted oxidation processes. This is where the glass marbles come into play. By carefully placing them in the fermentation vessel, the resulting space between the forming wine and the rim of the vessel is filled. This prevents contact with air and protects the wine from oxidation damage. Moreover, the glass marbles allow precise control over the bung, as you can vary the amount of glass marbles according to the fill level in the vessel.

Fermentation vessel

The fermentation vessel is a container in which the fermentation of the wine takes place. It can be made of different materials, such as glass, plastic or stainless steel. Most importantly, the fermentation vessel must seal well and provide enough space for the fermentation of the wine.

Figure 1: Fermentation vessel

Presser

The presser is an important piece of equipment for extracting the juice from the fruit. Depending on the type of fruit, you can use the presser for apples (quartered), pears (quartered), cherries, strawberries, raspberries, grapes and other types of berries. It allows efficient juice extraction and is indispensable, especially for larger quantities of fruit.

Figure 2: Press

Berry crusher

The berry crusher is specially designed for processing apples, pears and other stoneless fruit. It crushes the fruit to make it easier to squeeze out the juice.

Figure 3: Berry crusher

Juicer

The juicer is a versatile tool that can be used for all types of fruit. It allows you to extract juice quickly and efficiently and is particularly practical when you want to use different types of fruit.

Choosing these tools carefully and using them correctly is crucial to the success of your winemaking. Be sure to use high-quality materials and to clean and maintain the equipment regularly. To extract the juice from the fruit, it is adequate to use either a presser, berry grinder or juicer. It all depends on the fruit you want to process.

Figure 4: Juicer

3. Space

Choosing the right space for winemaking is relevant to ensure the quality and taste of the wine.

Fermentation room

The fermentation room is the place where the fermentation of the wine takes place. It is here that the yeasts transform the sugar contained in the fruit into alcohol and carbon dioxide, which makes the wine tasty and alcoholic. The following conditions must be observed for an optimal fermentation room:

- Ventilation: A ventilated fermentation room is advantageous to ensure sufficient oxygen supply during fermentation. If the room does not have natural ventilation, artificial ventilation can be provided by fans or similar means.
- Room temperature: The ideal room temperature for the fermentation room is between 15 °C and 25 °C. The yeast works most effectively at this temperature and converts the sugar into alcohol. A temperature that is too low can slow down or even stop fermentation, while a temperature that is too high can cause undesirable changes in taste.
- Darkening: Ideally, it should be possible to darken the fermentation room. This is important because light can

interfere with the fermentation process and cause un-desirable chemical reactions in the wine. If a darkened room is not available, the carboy or vessel can also be protected from light by appropriate means, such as blankets or cloths.

- Examples for the fermentation room: Suitable areas for the fermentation room include the boiler room, gar-ages or laundry rooms. These places often provide the necessary room temperature and the option of dark-ening to ensure ideal conditions for the fermentation of the wine.

Storage room

The storage room is the place where the wine can mature and develop its characteristic aromas. This is where the wine rests as it slowly reaches its peak.

- Humidity: The humidity in the storage room should ide-ally be between 60 and 70 %. Adequate humidity pre-vents the cork from drying out and thus undesirable ox-idation of the wine. This keeps the taste of the wine in-tact and preserves its quality.
- Room temperature: The ideal room temperature for the storage room is between 8 and 12 °C. In a cool room, the wine can mature slowly and develop an op-timal balance of its aromas. Too high a temperature,

on the other hand, can lead to premature ageing and changes in taste.

- Darkening: Similar to the fermentation room, darkening is also favourable in the storage room to protect the wine from harmful light. UV radiation, in particular, can have a negative effect on the wine and lead to undesirable chemical reactions.
- Suitable locations for the storage room are cool, dark cellars or pantries. Such places often provide the right climatic conditions for the wine to mature and allow for a slow and controlled development of its aromas.

Summary:

The right premises for winemaking are important to produce a delicious and high-quality wine. The fermentation room should provide a ventilated environment with a room temperature of 15 to 25 °C and, ideally, the option of darkening. For the storage room, a humidity of 60 to 70 % and a cool room temperature of 8 to 12 °C are desirable, also with the option of darkening.

4. Things to know about yeast

Yeast, a fungal growth, is a crucial player in winemaking and plays a central role in the conversion of sugars into alcohol and carbon dioxide during the fermentation process. Although microscopic and barely visible to the naked eye, yeast's effect on wine is immense. Yeast belongs to the group of fungi that reproduce by sprouting, which distinguishes it from other types of fungi. Their tiny size makes them invisible to the naked eye unless they are in large clusters, as is the case with baker's yeast. This ability to multiply by sprouting makes yeast an extremely efficient microorganism in winemaking. The main role of yeast in winemaking is to convert the sugars in the fruit into alcohol and carbon dioxide. This process, known as fermentation, is essential to the production of wine and gives it its characteristic alcohol content and properties. Yeasts are differentiated according to their ability to ferment sugars into alcohol. Some yeast strains can tolerate higher alcohol concentrations than others. These differences in alcohol tolerance influence the fermentation process and the final composition of the wine. The shape of the yeast cells can vary. Wine yeast has an elongated, elliptical shape, while brewer's yeast has a round shape. These differences can affect the properties and behaviour of the yeast strains during the fermentation process.

4.1 Yeast types

Pure-breeding yeasts

Pure-breeding yeasts are often used in modern wine production. Pure-breeding yeasts are specially bred yeast strains that enable controlled fermentation. By using pure-breeding yeasts, winemakers can better control the fermentation process and specifically develop the desired aromas and characteristics of the wine. Pure-breeding yeasts are available in both liquid and dry form. Both forms have their advantages and disadvantages, and the choice often depends on the winemaker's individual preferences and the specific requirements of the winemaking process.

Wild yeasts

Wild yeasts are natural yeast strains that are naturally present in the environment, for example on the surface of the grape skin. In some traditional winemaking processes, wild yeasts are used to give the wine a unique local flavour. However, the use of wild yeasts also carries the risk of unpredictable results and undesirable flavour changes.

Kahm yeasts

Kahm yeasts are undesirable yeast strains that can sometimes appear during the fermentation process. They can form on the surface of the wine and lead to unpleasant aromas and flavour changes. Proper hygiene and control of the fermentation room are necessary to minimise the occurrence of kahm yeasts.

4.2 What are the different types of yeast?

4.2.1   Yeast varieties for sweet wines

Sweet wines are known for their enticing sweetness, intriguing aromas and diverse flavour nuances. An important factor that determines these characteristic features is the choice of the right yeast variety during the fermentation process.

Sherry yeast

Sherry is a versatile sweet wine with a wide range of flavour profiles. The type of yeast used in sherry production helps determine the specific flavours and alcohol content of the wine. Sherry yeast can be used for a variety of fruits, including gooseberry and rosehip, and usually has an alcohol content of 12 to 15 % vol.

Haut Sauternes yeast

Haut Sauternes is an enticingly sweet wine. The yeast can be used to make elderberry, quince and rhubarb wines. The type of yeast used in the production of Haut Sauternes shapes the flavour profile and alcohol content of the wine, which is usually between 12 and 16 % vol.

Port wine yeast

Port is one of the most famous sweet wines in the world. A variety of exquisite fruits, such as elderberry, apricot, strawberry, rosehip, raspberry, gooseberry, mirabelle, plum, cranberry, quince, rhubarb, sour cherry and sloe, develop their full potential when fermented with port wine yeast. The choice of yeast variety for port wine production contributes significantly to the complexity of the wine, which usually has an alcohol content of 12 to 15 % vol.

Malaga yeast

Malaga is an enticing sweet wine with a rich array of flavours. The type of yeast used in the production of Malaga influences the wine's characteristic flavours. Apricot, strawberry, rosehip, mirabelle plum and cranberry are excellent for fermentation, and the result is a wine with an alcohol content of 12 to 15 % vol.

Tokay yeast

Tokay, also known as Tokaji, is a delicious sweet wine with an alcohol content of 10 to 16 % vol. The type of yeast used in tokay production is instrumental in balancing the sweetness and aroma of the wine.

Samos yeast

Samos is a sweet wine that comes from the fertile vineyards of the Greek island of Samos. The type of yeast used in the production of Samos determines the unique flavour nuances of this captivating wine, which usually has an alcohol content of 10 to 16 % vol.

4.2.2   Yeast varieties for semi-sweet wines

Semi-sweet wines are characterised by their gentle sweetness and delicate aromas, which tantalise the palate and offer a pleasant lightness. The choice of the right yeast variety is decisive in the production of these semi-sweet wines, as it determines the characteristic flavour profiles and the alcohol content.

Steinberg yeast

Steinberg is a delicious semi-sweet wine with an alcohol content of 8 to 10 % vol. The yeast used in the production of Steinberg brings out the characteristic aromas of this refreshing wine. Steinberg yeast is perfect for making wine from a variety of fruits, including apple, pear, plum, white grape and currant.

Bordeaux yeast

Bordeaux is a famous wine with complex aromas and an alcohol content of around 15 % vol. The type of yeast used in the production of Bordeaux influences the flavours of this rich and complex wine. Red grapes and blackberries are excellent for fermentation.

Burgundy yeast

Burgundy is a seductive semi-sweet wine with an alcohol content of about 15 % vol. The yeast used in the production of Burgundy helps to develop the elegant aromas of this captivating wine. Burgundy yeast can be used in a variety of ways, for example for the fermentation of sloe, blackberry, blueberry, raspberry, plum, elderberry and sour cherry.

4.2.3 Yeast varieties for dry wines

Dry wines are characterised by their fine elegance, balanced acidity and subtle aromas. The choice of the right yeast variety has a major role to play in the production of these dry wines, as it has a decisive influence on the characteristic flavour profiles and the alcohol content.

Bernkastel yeast

Bernkastel is a magical dry wine with an alcohol content of 6 to 8 % vol. The type of yeast used in the production of Bernkastel determines the characteristic aromas of this elegant wine. Apple, fig, rosehip, rhubarb, sultana, gooseberry and grape are suitable for fermentation.

Zeltinger yeast

Zeltinger is a captivating dry wine with an alcohol content of 6 to 8 % vol. The yeast variety used in the production of Zeltinger helps to develop the subtle aromas of this enticing wine. The fruits apple, redcurrant, rosehip, rhubarb and grape are particularly suitable for this yeast variety.

The classification of pure yeasts into 'sweet wines', 'semi-sweet wines' and 'dry wines' is not based on the actual sugar content, but rather on their ability to produce glycerol during the fermentation process. Glycerol, also known as sugar alcohol or alditol, is the simplest trivalent alcohol. Glycerol, a colourless, odourless, sweet-tasting liquid labelled E422 in foods, as well as in other applications such as shoe polish or antifreeze, has a mild sweetening effect on the taste of high-alcohol wines, regardless of the actual sweetness of the wine. It gives the wine a thicker consistency and ensures that the taste lingers longer on the palate. There is still a misconception that yeast gives wine a special character. In fact, the use of different yeasts cannot fundamentally change the character of a grape or fruit wine. The fruit bouquet determines the character of the wine, while the fermentation bouquet of the yeast can only support and enhance this character. Furthermore, the pasteurisation of the juice before the addition of pure yeast in order to kill wild yeasts and only carry out a fermentation with a certain yeast strain is not recommended, as the wine becomes monotonous and loses its richness. Wild yeasts can play a special role in the formation of substances that are important for the development of the stock's bouquet.

5. What yeast nutrients are there?

Rightly understood, yeasts need sufficient nutrients for their multiplication, or so-called sprouting. If these nutrients are not present in sufficient form, this can inhibit yeast sprouting or, in the worst case, even lead to a fermentation standstill, which is called 'stuck fermentation'. Stuck fermentation can be a serious problem for a winemaker, as it leads to undesirable results. On the one hand, the sugar in the wine remains unfermented, which leads to a higher residual sugar content and makes the wine sweeter than planned, and on the other hand, there is the risk that the wine becomes unstable and undesirable chemical reactions can occur. To avoid fermentation stoppages, it is crucial for winemakers to provide the yeasts with sufficient nutrients. This includes important elements such as nitrogen compounds, phosphates, vitamins and trace elements. These nutrients are essential for the healthy growth and reproduction of the yeasts. Winemakers can optimise the nutrient supply of the yeasts by adding special yeast nutrient salts or yeast nutrient solutions. These contain a balanced mixture of nutrients that are necessary for the yeasts during the fermentation process. This ensures that the yeasts have the best possible conditions to do their job efficiently. When using preparations and additives during winemaking, it is always advisable to follow the manufacturer's recommendations carefully. Manufacturers provide recommendations regarding the dosage and application of the preparations in order to achieve optimal results and to avoid excessive addition, which could potentially have a negative effect on the wine. Winemakers should therefore always read the manufacturer's recommendations carefully and act accordingly to ensure the quality and safety of their wine.

Needs of the yeast cell

Vitamins	Nitrogen-containing compounds	Minerals	Lipids	Stereols
Increasing the speed of growth	"Reproduction engine", increasing amino acid metabolism	Provision of enzyme co-factors	Stabilization and increase of cell membrane transport of cell growth	

		Inactive yeasts	Yeast autolysates	Yeast cell wall/yeast bark

- Thiamine (B_1)
- Partially by yeast cell wall preparations
- Grapes contaminated with rot
- Bentonite fining
- In the first third of fermentation

- Ammonium sulfate (DAS) ((NH_4)$_2SO_4$), Diammonium hydrogen phosphate (DAP) ((NH_4)$_2HPO_4$) under-supplied musts
- Bocksern occurring during fermentation
- before or during fermentation

Inactive yeasts

- Improves rehydration of dry yeast by increasing yeast resistance
- Improving the shelf life and aroma stability of white and rosé wines
- At the beginning, during, towards the end

Yeast autolysates

- Formation of higher alcohols and their volatile fruit esters by the yeast
- Increasing the aromatic complexity and intensity of aromas typical of grape varieties
- Increased internal surface area for better fermentation performance
- After the first third of fermentation

Yeast cell wall/yeast bark

- Increased internal surface area for better fermentation performance
- Adsorption power against fermentation-inhibiting substances
- A third at the beginning of fermentation, the rest towards the end

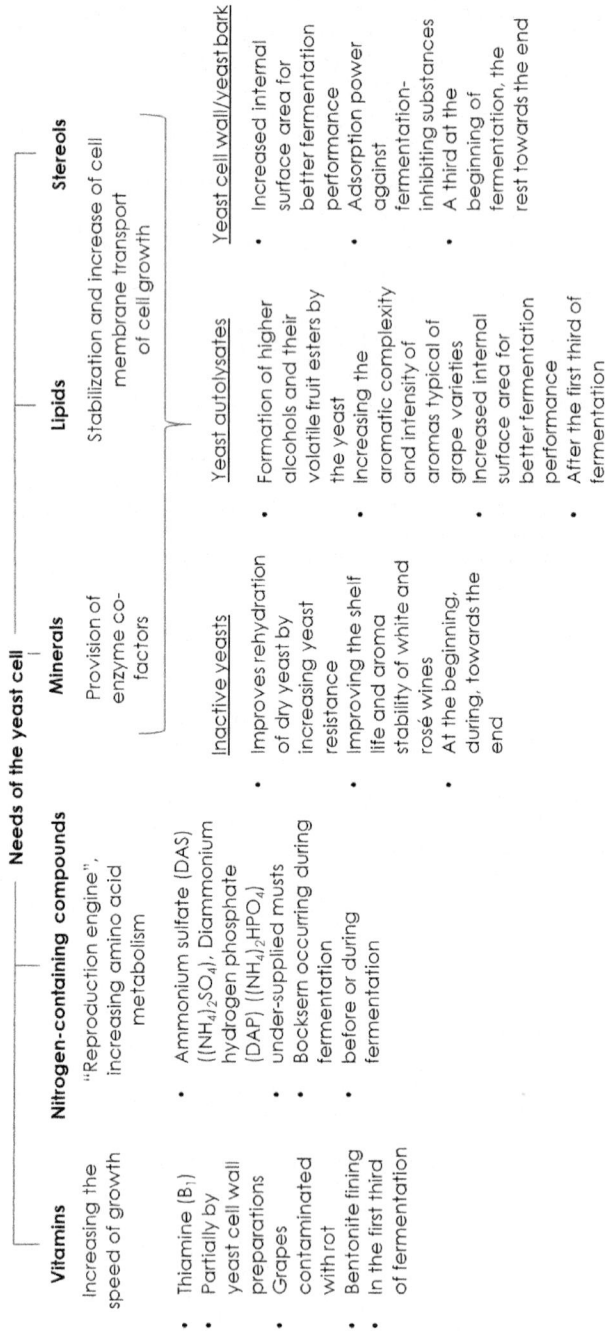

Figure 5: Nutrient requirements of the yeast cell

26

6. Preparing a fermentation starter

Making delicious wine starts with a fermentation starter, which brings the yeasts to life and starts the fermentation process. Here is a simple guide to making your own fermentation starter for wine making:

Ingredients:

- 0.5 l naturally cloudy/clear apple juice or clear grape juice
- 0.5 g yeast nutrient salt
- 50 g sugar
- Pure yeast (either a small bottle of liquid yeast or 0.1 g dry yeast, more if needed, depending on your requirements)

Instructions:

1. Choose a suitable vessel with enough space for the foaming process of fermentation. Make sure it is clean and sterilised to create the best environment for the yeasts.
2. Pour the naturally cloudy or clear apple juice or grape juice into the vessel.
3. Add the yeast nutrient salt to give the yeasts the nutrients they need to multiply. This helps to develop a healthy and active yeast culture.

27

4. Add the sugar to the vessel. The sugar serves as a food source for the yeasts.

5. If you are using liquid yeast, shake the vial well to ensure that the yeast is well distributed. Pour all the liquid yeast into the fermentation starter.

6. If dry yeast has been selected, add 0.1 g dry yeast, or more if necessary, to the fermentation starter.

7. Stir the ingredients well to make sure everything is well mixed.

8. Fill the fermentation tube with water and place it on the fermentation vessel with a rubber adapter piece. (see figure 6: Fermentation starter).

9. Leave the fermentation starter to stand at room temperature. In one to three days, the fermentation process should start, as indicated by the formation of foam or bubbles.

10. Once fermentation is in full swing, you can use the starter to add inoculants to your must or wine. Liquid yeasts usually require 50-100 ml of fermentation starter per 10 litres of wine.

Making a fermentation starter is an important step in wine-making to ensure that the yeasts are active and healthy, thus allowing a successful fermentation process. By following these simple instructions and being careful about the amount of yeast you use, you can optimise your winemaking and create delicious wines with full-bodied aromas and balanced flavour profiles.

Figure 6: fermentation starter

7. Sulphur process

The use of sulphur in winemaking is an important practice to improve the quality and shelf life of wine. However, it is advisable to keep the use of sulphur as low as possible, as excessive use can have negative effects on taste and health. Here are some important aspects of sulphurisation in winemaking:

Why is sulphur used?

- It kills off troublesome microorganisms in the wine that can cause undesirable flavours and off-tones.
- It prevents the spread of oxidation enzymes that can prematurely age the wine.
- Sulphur helps clarify the wine by reducing suspended solids and turbidity.
- It stabilises the wine, which allows it to be stored for longer.

What is used for sulphurisation?

- Sulphur sticks are used if only the fermentation vessel is to be sulphurised.
- Potassium disulphite ($K_2S_2O_5$) is used to make a 2 percent sulphur solution. To do this, dissolve 40 g of potassium disulphite and 2 g of citric acid or lactic acid in 1 l of water.

Important notes:

- It is crucial to always clean the equipment just before use to avoid contaminating the wine.

- It is important not to inhale sulphur vapours as they can be harmful to health. Sulphur can also be harmful to health if taken orally. In larger quantities, it has a negative effect on the vitamin balance in the body. Quite a few people even have an allergic reaction to sulphur additives.

- Without sulphur, winemaking requires an extremely careful and clinically hygienic approach. It is essential to use only the best and healthiest fruit for the wine to ensure optimal quality. In addition, all operations must be carried out swiftly and precisely to avoid unwanted contamination. Since wine without sulphur is less protected and more susceptible to oxidation and microbial spoilage, it is advisable not to store it for more than two years. Longer storage can lead to the wine losing quality and undesirable flavour changes. Without sulphur, wines can retain their natural character better. However, it requires a great deal of experience and knowledge to successfully implement this method of winemaking.

What is sulphurised?

- The equipment to be used is sulphurised to ensure a clean working environment.
- The quantity of fruit juice or must is sulphurised with 1 g of potassium disulphite per 10 litres. It is possible to halve the dose in order to reduce the health risk. However, it should be individually checked whether the desired effect still occurs, depending on how cleanly the work was done.
- The young wine, which has been drawn off the yeast after the first fermentation, is sulphurised with 1 g of potassium disulphite per 10 litres.
- Before being bottled, the wine is sulphurised with 1 g of potassium disulphite
  per 10 litres.
- If the wine has to be filtered, it is also sulphurised with 1 g of potassium disulphite per 10 litres.

The correct use of sulphur in winemaking is a careful balance between the positive effects and possible negative effects. By following recommended dosages and conscientiously maintaining winemaking hygiene, winemakers can improve the quality of their wines while ensuring that health considerations are taken into account. Sulphurisation is an important practice that enables winemakers to produce wines of the highest quality with a long shelf life.

8. Sugar addition and acidity

Adding sugar during winemaking can increase the subsequent alcohol level in the finished wine, compared to just fermenting the sugars naturally present in the fruit. During fermentation, the yeasts convert the sugar into alcohol and carbon dioxide. The amount of sugar available to the yeasts determines the alcohol content of the finished wine. When the yeasts naturally ferment the available sugar, the alcohol content is generally lower because the amount of sugar is limited. Adding additional sugar to the must or fruit juice before or during fermentation increases the amount of sugar available to the yeasts. This leads to the yeasts fermenting more sugar and consequently producing more alcohol. Thus, the alcohol content of the wine will be higher than in the case of a fermentation without additional sugar. This method is sometimes used by winemakers to produce wines with a higher alcohol content when the fruit has a low natural sugar content or when a certain alcohol content is desired. The addition of sugar can help to achieve a desired flavour style or strength of wine. However, it is important to dose the addition of sugar carefully, as excessive use can lead to an unbalanced wine. Too much alcohol can dominate the taste of the wine and mask the fruit aromas. Therefore, the dosage of additional sugar is an art that requires experience and finesse.

Variant 1 – For beginner

If you are a beginner in winemaking and want to get started without special equipment, there is a simple method for making your own wine. Note that this method may not be as precise, but may be sufficient to get you started. Making a great-tasting wine requires a basic understanding of some important factors:

- Tartaric acidity: A palatable wine typically has about 7 g/l of tartaric acid. During fermentation there may be a loss of about 1–2 g/l.
- Adding sugar for increased alcohol content: If you want to increase the alcohol content of your wine, you can add sugar. A rough rule of thumb is that 20 g of sugar per 1 litre of wine will increase the alcohol content by about 1 percent by volume.
- Ratio of sugar to sugar water: If you dissolve 1 kg of sugar in water, you will get about 0.6 l of sugar water.

Fruit juice	Acidity [g/l]	Sugar content [g/l]	Fruit juice yield [kg/l]
Apple	8	100	1,5
Blackberry	8	40	1,25
Strawberry	10	40	1,25
Rosehips	19	negligible	1,7
Blueberry	8	40	1,25
Currant, red	23	20	1,43
Currant, black	26	20	1,43
Currant, white	20	20	1,43
Rhubarb	12	negligible	1,7
Sour cherry	16	40	1,5
Sloes	35	negligible	1,7
Gooseberry	16	20	1,43

Figure 7: Overview of acidity, sugar content and fruit juice yield of the individual fruits

In the following, the example of a currant wine will be used to show how the required amount of water and sugar is calculated. This procedure can be applied to any wine.

Water addition

Calculating the water to be added using the rule of three allows you to find out the amount of water needed.

1 l currant juice = 26 g/l acid (see figure 7)

x l currant juice = 8 g/l acid (ideal acidity)

$$\frac{1\,l * 26\,\frac{g}{l}}{8\,\frac{g}{l}} = x = 3.25\,l$$

Multiply to 3.25 litres by adding 2.25 litres of water. This step is crucial to achieve the desired volume of wine and to dilute the liquid to the right concentration. The addition of the water brings the wine to the desired final volume without compromising the taste or quality. It is important to measure the amount of water accurately to avoid over- or underdosing and to keep the wine in perfect balance. This meticulous multiplication ensures that the wine develops the desired aromas and characteristics and that the final product is harmonious in taste.

Sugar addition

The calculation of the amount of sugar to be added is crucial if you want to make a wine with a certain alcohol content. It is important to consider the sugar volume, as sugar dissolves in water and thus influences the total volume.

Let's say you want to make a currant wine with 11 % vol. of alcohol. You have already brought the wine must to the correct acidity. In this example, this corresponds to a total volume of 3.25 litres. The basic sugar content of the fruit can be seen in figure 7. Since currants already have 20 g/l sugar, all you need to prepare an 11 % vol. wine is to add sugar for 10 % vol.

$$20\frac{g}{l} * 10 \% \ vol.* 3.25 \ l = \textbf{650 g sugar}$$

It is important to take the sugar volume into account, because if it is not taken into account, the acidity would be suppressed excessively. Here, 1 kg of sugar in a dissolved state corresponds to about 0.6 l.

$$0.650 \ kg \ sugar * 0.6 \ l = \textbf{0.39 l sugar volume}$$

$$3.25 \ l \ wine - 1 \ l \ juice - 0.39 \ l \ sugar \ volume$$
$$= \textbf{1.86 l} (\approx \textbf{1.9 l}) \textbf{ water}$$

Summary:

You get 3.25 l of wine from 1.43 kg of currants. To achieve the desired alcohol content of 11 % vol., add 650 g of sugar to the juice. In addition, 1.86 l of water is added to the juice to ensure optimal acidity and to take into account the natural reduction during fermentation. This careful process ensures that the wine has a balanced taste and the desired characteristics. Calculating the amount of water to be added, taking into account the volume of sugar, is an important step in producing a high-quality wine.

Variant 2 - For advanced winemakers

In the fascinating world of winemaking, measuring sugar content is fundamental to control the alcohol content of the wine and also to determine the perfect time for harvesting.

Refractometer

The refractometer is a measuring instrument used in winemaking to determine the sugar content in must or grape juice. It works on the basis of light refraction and measures the refractive index of the juice. The higher the sugar content in the juice, the more the light is refracted. Based on the measurement results, the winemaker can read the sugar content in degrees Oechsle. This is crucial to determine the right time for harvesting and to control the alcohol formation in the wine later on. The refractometer is a practical and efficient tool that provides the winemaker with valuable information for winemaking. When using a refractometer, there is one important factor to consider: The temperature at which the measurement is taken. Sugar content is usually measured at a calibration temperature of 20 °C, as this is where the meter is most accurate. If the temperature is higher or lower than 20 °C, an appropriate correction must be made to obtain accurate measurement results. At temperatures above 20 °C, 0.2 °Oe (degrees Oechsle units) must be added to the measured value for each degree Celsius. Conversely, at temperatures below 20 °C, 0.2 °Oe must be subtracted per degree Celsius. This precise correction allows you to accurately determine the actual sugar content in the must and keep an eye on fermentation. The 0 °Oe value marks the point at which fermentation is complete and the wine has reached its desired alcohol content. It is a significant milestone in winemaking and shows that your diligent work is bearing fruit.

It is important to note that the sugar content can only be measured as long as fermentation has not started. The conversion of sugar into alcohol causes a reduction in the must weight over time. Therefore, it is advisable to measure the sugar content before fermentation starts in order to obtain accurate results. Otherwise, measure the residual sugar content still present.

Determining the optimal harvest time therefore requires a trained eye and an understanding of the relationships between temperature, sugar content and fermentation. With the refractometer as a reliable aid, you can further refine the quality of your wines.

Fruit	Quality [°Oe]			
	bad	moderate	good	very good
Apple	≈24	≈40	≈56	≈72
Blackberry	≈24	≈32	≈48	≈56
Strawberry	≈32	≈48	≈64	≈72
Cherry	≈24	≈32	≈56	≈64
Grape	≈24	≈48	≈72	≈88

Figure 8: Harvest time of some fruits

If you read a value of 72 °Oe for an apple with the help of the refractometer, then the perfect harvest time has come.

Conversion of °Oe to g/l and % vol.

An example to illustrate the calculation of alcohol content in grams/litre (g/l). Assume that the measured value on the Oechsle scale is 100 °Oe. We now want to determine the alcohol content in grams per litre (g/l). The formula below was obtained by linear regression (from figure 9).

$$Alcohol_{\frac{g}{l}} (°Oe) = (1.275 * °Oe) - 18$$

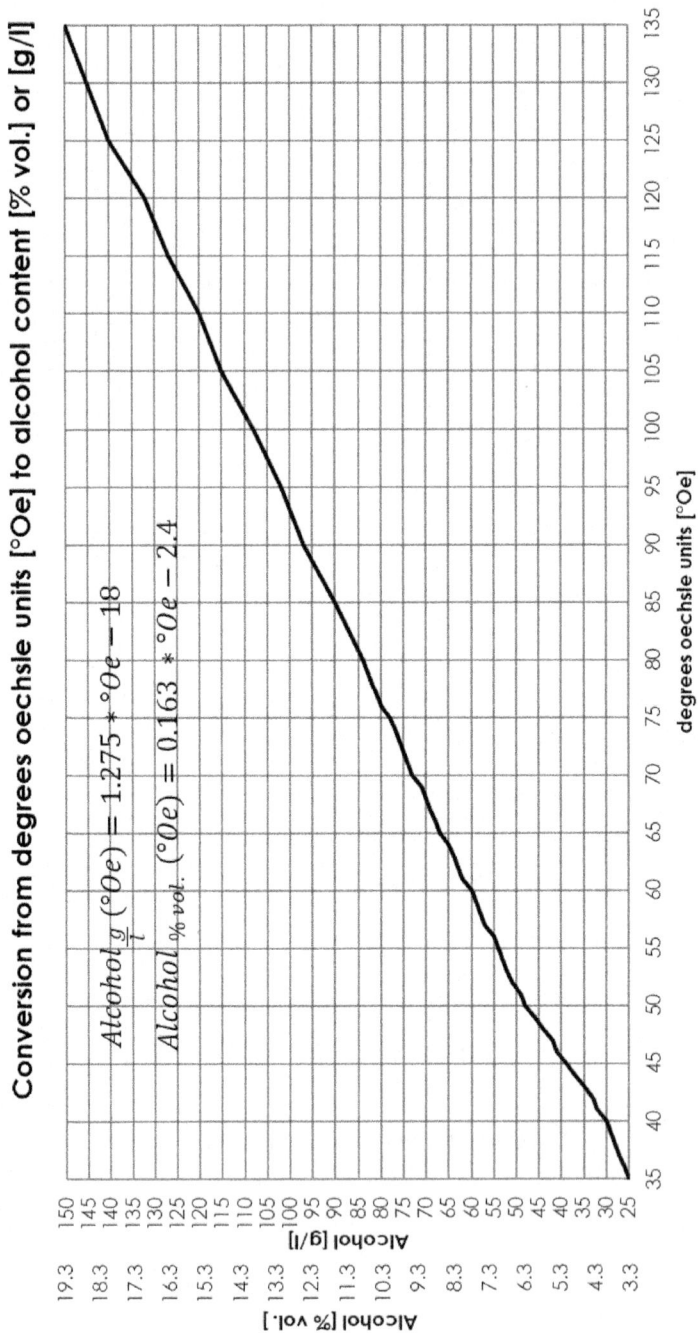

Figure 9: Conversion °Oe in g/l and % vol.

According to the formula in figure 9, we insert the measured value:

$$(1.275 * 100\,°Oe) - 18\,l = 109.5\,\frac{g}{l}$$

This means that the wine in this example has an alcohol content of about 109.5 grams per litre.

To calculate the alcohol content in volume percent [% vol.], we use the formula below, which is also obtained by linear regression.

$$Alcohol_{\%\,vol.} = (0.163 * °Oe) - 2.4$$

$$(0.163 * 100) - 2.4 = 13.9\,\%\,vol.$$

This means that the wine in this example has an alcohol content of about 13.9 % vol. These calculations allow you to accurately determine the alcohol content of your wine and add the desired alcohol content to your creations. Knowing the alcohol content is crucial to producing wines with perfect flavour nuances and the ideal alcohol content. With this method, you can determine the initial sugar content of your must, and then, using the calculation method shown, determine the sugar you need to add to obtain a wine with the desired alcohol content.

Figure 10: Refractometer

Measuring acidity

Measuring acidity is essential to control and refine the quality and taste of your wine. With the help of an acidometer, you can determine the total acidity of the juice as well as the amount of free sulphurous acids. In addition, you can use litmus paper, which acts as an indicator for acids and bases and displays the pH value of the juice. Blue lye is also needed. Accurate measurement of acidity is a critical step in winemaking and helps you optimise the character and quality of your wine.

Procedure

To determine the acidity of the juice, a glass cylinder (acidometer) is used, which is filled with the juice up to the zero mark on the scale. The exact marking must be adhered to. When taking the reading, it is important to always hold the glass cylinder at eye level in order to obtain accurate results. To add the blue lye, hold the bottle with the nozzle cap facing downwards diagonally over the opening of the measuring cylinder and carefully press a few millilitres of lye into the cylinder with your fingers. Then close the cylinder with your thumb and carefully tip it over. Before removing the thumb, wipe it along the edge to allow the liquid to flow back. Repeat this process of letting the lye flow in, repeatedly closing the cylinder opening with your thumb until the colour changes to dark green. Then hold the cylinder at eye level and wait until the liquid adhering to the inside wall of the cylinder has run together to read the result. If too much lye has been added by mistake and the colour has already turned blue, make a note of this number and repeat the process with more careful additions. When analysing very dark juices or wines for acidity, it is recommended that they should be diluted. The value determined must then be multiplied by the dilution factor to obtain the correct result.

With a little practice and no prior knowledge, accuracies of ± 0.5 g acidity can be achieved and this is perfectly adequate for practical use.

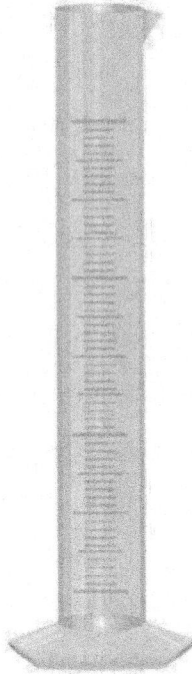

Figure 11: Acidometer

9. Vinometer

The vinometer is an inexpensive instrument for the approximate determination of the alcohol content in mashes, wines and musts. It is based on the principle of surface tension and enables the alcohol content to be measured quickly and easily in % vol.

Basic rules for determining the alcohol content:

- The vinometer must be clean to ensure accurate results.
- The sample must be free of turbidity to prevent distortion.
- The temperature of the vinometer and the sample should be around 20 °C in order to obtain optimum measurements.

This is how the vinometer works:

Step 1: Perform calibration with distilled water

- Fill the vinometer with distilled water and ensure that it is free of turbidity.
- Carrying out at least three calibration procedures is recommended. To complete the calibration, go to step 3. Make sure that the value read is 0. If not, correct your future measurement by this amount. If you have

already carried out several calibration procedures, continue with step 2.

Step 2: Fill the sample into the funnel without bubbles

- Carefully fill the sample to be measured into the funnel of the vinometer without any air pockets until it has reached the lower end.

Step 3: Turn the vinometer upside down and place it on a flat surface

- Close the lower end of the vinometer with your finger.
- Carefully turn the vinometer over and place it on a flat surface.
- Once the equilibrium of forces has been established, you can read off the alcohol content in % vol.
- Make sure that the reading angle is approximately 90 degrees to avoid parallax errors (misalignment).

Note: It is advisable to carry out several calibration procedures to ensure a high level of accuracy.

You can use this simple but effective instrument to determine the alcohol content of your mashes, wines and musts. Please note, however, that this method only provides an approximation and is not an exact measurement. For a more precise analysis of the alcohol content, it is advisable to use professional measuring methods or laboratory tests. Nevertheless, the vinometer offers a quick and inexpensive way to obtain a rough overview of the alcohol content of your wines and to monitor the development of your wine production.

10. Anti-gelling agents

Pectins, which are found in fruit, play an important role in the structure of the pulp, as they hold the pulp cells together and prevent the release of juice, flavours and colours. This is important for the quality and flavour of the wine. When fruit is processed into mash, the mash should normally stand for a long time so that the splitting process of the pectinase (enzyme) can take place effectively. However, in order to shorten the standing time of the mash and minimise the oxidation of the must, an anti-gelling agent, such as pectinase, is often added. This makes the mash thinner and easier to press. The addition of pectinase causes an increased release of flavours and colours from the mash. In addition, natural cloudy substances settle more quickly, which leads to a clearer colour of wine. This enables faster and more efficient winemaking. However, it is important to note that anti-gelling agents are very temperature-dependent. They are ineffective at temperatures below 10 °C, while they are killed at temperatures above 55 °C. In order to break down the pectins, the mash should rest at around 15 °C for around 15 hours. Increasing the temperature by 10 °C would halve the mash's resting time. It is therefore important to follow the exact information and instructions for the anti-gelling agent used. After the anti-gelling agent has taken effect, the mash can be pressed to extract the juice. The anti-gelling agent can also be used to clarify the wine, as it primarily breaks down the pectins to give the wine a clear colour. The use of anti-gelling agents enables more effective winemaking and helps the wine to develop an appealing colour, intense aroma and flavourful character.

11. Bentonite fining

Fort Benton, a finely ground swelling clay named after its main location in the US state of Montana, is used as an effective aid in winemaking. Due to its large surface area, the swollen clay binds proteins, clouding substances and flavours in the wine, causing them to sink to the bottom and thus clarify the wine. Another advantage of bentonite is that it can conceal faults in the wine. Bentonite can be used to mask undesirable aromas and flavours, particularly in the case of very rotten grapes. However, it is important to emphasise that the use of bentonite in winemaking should not be seen as a substitute for a high-quality fruit harvest. It is always advisable to use high-quality grapes to achieve the best results. Although bentonite is an effective method of clarifying wine, there is a possibility that it can lead to noticeable loss of flavour and colour, especially if overdosed. For this reason, precise dosing and application of bentonite is essential, depending on the specific batch of wine and the desired results. Bentonite can be used in different stages during the winemaking process. In the first stage, it can be used for fining the must to remove grape proteins, tannins and amino acids, and to clarify the must. In later stages of the winemaking process, such as between the first and second pressing, the use of bentonite can be particularly useful to further clarify and stabilise the wine. Overall, bentonite is a valuable aid in winemaking, helping to produce clear, flavourful and appealing wines. However, the correct use and dosage of bentonite requires experience and sensitivity in order to achieve the desired results and not negatively influence the character of the wine. It is therefore also advisable to follow the specific instructions and recommendations when using bentonite.

12. Pre-mashing

Pre-treatment of the fruit before pressing is an important step in winemaking, which facilitates the subsequent pressing of the fruit and increases the juice yield. This pre-treatment is also known as pre-fermentation and involves crushing the fruit in order to open the still-closed cells and allow the juice to flow out more easily. At the same time, this process destroys pectins and mucilage in the fruit, which favours the subsequent processing and fermentation of the juice. The first step in pre-treatment is to place the crushed or ground fruit in a fermentation vessel with a large opening. This fermentation vessel can be made of plastic, glass, clay or stainless steel, and should be fitted with a fermentation tube to facilitate the fermentation process. It is important to only fill the fermentation vessel to about 2/3 of its capacity, as the contents increase in volume due to the development of carbon dioxide during fermentation and form a so-called cap. If necessary, sulphurisation can also be carried out at this stage to kill off unwanted microorganisms. In the next step, the pure yeast is added to the fermentation vessel to initiate fermentation. An anti-gelling agent can also be added to make the liquid thinner and achieve a better juice yield. The fermentation process is supported by regularly pushing the resulting cap back into the liquid, which is done several times a day. It is important to always thoroughly clean the pushing tool before use to prevent contamination. The mashing process usually takes one to three days, depending on the type of fruit and the desired result. Once this process is complete, the juice is drawn off and placed in a carboy that has previously been sulphurised. The remaining solid parts of the fruit are then pressed, and the juice obtained is also added to the carboy. The pre-treatment of the fruit by pre-fermentation is an essential step in winemaking in order to achieve an optimum juice yield and create the basis for a high-quality wine. By opening the cells and destroying pectins and mucilage, the juice is made more accessible, and fermentation can proceed more efficiently, resulting in a flavourful and clear wine.

13. Transfer to a new fermentation vessel

Separating the wine from sediments, also known as clarifying the wine, is another essential step in the winemaking process in order to obtain a clear and pure wine. After fermentation, a layer of dead yeast, turbidity and other particles forms at the bottom of the carboy, making the wine look cloudy and unclear. To separate the wine from these deposits, the carboy is carefully placed on a table to stir up as few deposits as possible from the bottom. A second vessel, ideally another sulphurised carboy, is placed further down so that there is a difference in height between the two vessels. In the next step, a clean tube is inserted up to a maximum of 1 cm above the sediment in the carboy. The wine is carefully drawn in with the other end of the tube, and as soon as the first liquid has reached the mouth, the tube is closed by hand, a clip or a tap. The tube is then inserted into the container below and the cap is opened. This allows the liquid to be exchanged between the two vessels, with the wine flowing into the second vessel and the sediment remaining in the carboy. It is important to minimise the amount of sediment transferred to the new container, as this could affect the clarification of the wine. Careful use of the hose is therefore necessary. Once the wine has been poured into the second container, the sediment can be strained through an appropriate filter. The filtered juice can then be returned to the carboy to continue fermentation. Clarifying the wine by separating sediments is an essential step in obtaining a clear and flavourful wine. The removal of turbidity and dead yeast not only makes the wine visually appealing, but also improves its flavour, as there are many undesirable particles in the sediments.

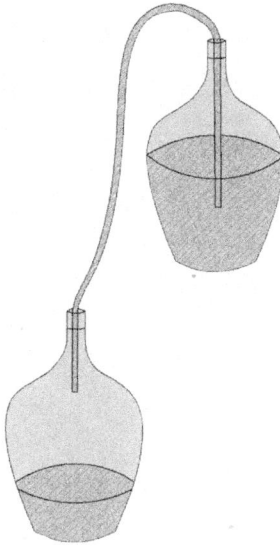

Figure 10: Transfer to a new fermentation vessel

14. Stuck fermentation

Stopping the yeast's activity of converting sugar into alcohol when there is still residual sugar can lead to a problem known as stuck wine. This can have various causes, such as an incorrect fermentation temperature (either too warm or too cold) or a vinegar spike caused by unclean working practices. Too much vinegar can lead to the wine only being able to be processed into vinegar, which is, of course, undesirable.

A few steps are required to correct a stuck wine:

1. If possible, a fermentation starter should be prepared two to three days in advance.

2. The stuck wine is drawn off from the yeast into a pot. The liquid is then heated to 65 °C and kept at this temperature for approx. 30 minutes. The pot should remain covered to minimise the loss of alcohol. The heating process also reliably kills any bacteria and germs that may be present.

3. After heating, the prepared fermentation starter is added to the wine. If no fermentation starter is available, 0.5 g of yeast nutrient salt and a fresh quantity of pure yeast can be added per 1 litre of wine instead.

These steps restart the fermentation in the stuck wine, and the yeast can convert the remaining sugar into alcohol. The correct implementation of these measures can save the stuck wine and give it the opportunity to become a fully fermented and drinkable wine. However, it is important to work carefully and cleanly to avoid the risk of vinegar taint.

15. Closure types

Natural cork stoppers

Natural corks, made from the bark of the cork oak, have long been a popular closure for wine bottles. They have both advantages and disadvantages that the wine industry and wine lovers alike must take into account. One of the most important advantages of natural corks is their ability to allow the wine to mature. The slightly porous structure of the cork allows the wine to interact with small amounts of oxygen, resulting in gentle oxidation. This oxidation allows the wine to develop over time and develop its aromas and flavours.

Figure 11: Natural cork stoppers

Many wines, especially high-quality and storable varieties, benefit from ageing in the bottle and gain in complexity and character. However, natural corks also have a significant disadvantage known as cork taint. The cork defect is caused by contamination of the cork with the chemical substance tri-chloroanisole (TCA). TCA is odourless and tasteless, but in tiny concentrations it can contaminate the wine with an unpleasant 'corky' smell and taste. This can significantly impair enjoyment of the wine and make it undrinkable. The cork defect occurs in a small number of corks, but it is nevertheless a risk that the wine industry always keeps an eye on.

Synthetic corks

Synthetic corks, made from materials such as sugar cane, are an alternative closure solution for wine bottles. They have been developed to avoid some of the disadvantages of natural corks, while still allowing or supporting the ageing process of the wine. Similar to natural corks, synthetic corks also allow low oxygen permeability, which allows the wine to oxidise gently and thus develop its aromas and flavours over time. This is particularly important for wines that require a certain ageing period in the bottle in order to develop their best characteristics. Another advantage of synthetic corks is their consistency and durability. Unlike natural corks, which can vary due to their natural origin and structure, synthetic corks offer consistent quality and are less susceptible to cork taint (TCA). This minimises the risk of cork-damaged wines and provides consumers with a reliable closure solution. Despite these advantages, synthetic corks also have a potential disadvantage. They can release foreign flavours into the wine, especially in the first few months after the bottle is sealed. This can affect the flavour of the wine and result in it not developing the desired character. It is important, therefore, to use high-quality synthetic corks specially developed for wines in order to minimise this risk.

Figure 12: Synthetic corks

Pressed cork stoppers

Press corks, also known as cork granulate press corks, are another closure solution for wine bottles. They consist of cork granulate that is pressed under pressure to form a closure. Pressed corks were developed to offer a more cost-effective alternative to natural corks, while still retaining the traditional look of a cork stopper. One advantage of pressed corks is their attractive price compared to natural corks. As they are made from granulated cork, they are cheaper to produce, which means that wineries and producers often see them as a more cost-effective option. This can be particularly advantageous for bulk bottling and for wines that do not require a long ageing period. Nevertheless, pressed cork stoppers have the same disadvantage as natural cork stoppers – they are susceptible to cork taint (TCA). TCA is a compound that results from contamination with chlorine-containing chemicals and causes a musty odour and taste in the wine. Although pressed corks are generally less susceptible to cork taint than natural corks, there is still some risk, especially if poor quality or contaminated cork granules are used.

Figure 13: Pressed cork stoppers

Glass corks

Glass corks are a modern closure solution for wine bottles in which a glass closure with aplastic stopper is used. This closure option also has both advantages and disadvantages for wine bottling. A major advantage of glass corks is that they are tasteless and odourless. In contrast to natural corks or some plastic closures, glass corks cannot transfer any foreign flavours or odours to the wine. This enables an unadulterated and pure taste experience, whereby the original flavours and characteristics are preserved. One disadvantage of glass corks is that they can cause reductive tones in the wine. Reductive tones occur when the wine does not come into sufficient contact with oxygen during storage. This can lead to undesirable flavours that give the wine a certain imbalance. It is important that glass corks are produced using sophisticated technology to regulate the passage of oxygen and minimise the risk of reductive tones.

Figure 14: Glass corks

Screw cap

The screw cap, also known as a screw top, is a closure mechanism for wine bottles that is made of aluminium. A major advantage of the screw cap is that it does not allow cork defects. Unlike natural corks and some synthetic or pressed corks, the screw cap is free from TCA, which is responsible for cork taint This virtually eliminates the risk of an unpleasant cork flavour in the wine, ensuring reliable and consistent wine quality. A disadvantage of the screw cap is that it can cause reductive tones in the wine. This can result in undesirable flavours that give the wine a certain imbalance.

It is important to note that nowadays screw caps are developed with special technologies to control oxygen ingress and minimise reductive tones. Modern screw caps therefore often provide a good balance between protection against cork failure and control of oxygen exposure.

However, the choice of closure remains a personal decision, taking into account various factors, such as the desired ageing process, wine profile and consumer preferences.

Note: Removal of mould spores in corks – A temperature of 65 °C sustained for approx. 30 minutes reliably kills vegetative forms of bacteria, yeasts and moist moulds. However, some bacteria are resistant to this temperature, but do not pose any danger as they cannot grow in an acidic environment.

Mould spores in a dry state and permanent forms of yeasts that can withstand temperatures of 90 °C to 100 °C are much more dangerous. It is therefore advisable to soak bottles and corks thoroughly beforehand in order to soak the spores and encourage germination. In this condition, the spores can withstand significantly lower temperatures, and can therefore be killed more effectively. In some cases, rinsing or soaking the bottles or corks in diluted sulphurous acid (0.5 to 1.5%) overnight may also be recommended to achieve sterilisation and eliminate unwanted microorganisms.

16. Pasteurisation

Pasteurisation is a process used in winemaking to increase the shelf life of wine and eliminate unwanted microorganisms. This process also prevents secondary fermentation in the bottle due to remaining yeast cultures, which minimises the risk of pressure build-up and bursting of the bottle or dislodging of the cork. Another advantage of pasteurisation is that it improves the taste of the wine. Heating during the pasteurisation process causes the wine to age artificially. As a result, pasteurised wines are stored on average three to six months longer than unpasteurised wines. Pasteurisation therefore allows even young wines to undergo a flavour maturation process and develop a rounder and more complex taste.

However, it is important to note that not all wines need to be pasteurised. The decision to pasteurise depends on several factors, including the style of the wine and the intended shelf life. Tart wines can benefit from pasteurisation, but it is not a mandatory requirement. Some winemakers deliberately choose not to pasteurise in order to promote the wine's natural ageing process and preserve specific flavour profiles.

Cork stoppers

The use of corks to seal wine bottles is a tried and tested method of protecting the wine from air and external influences and allowing it to mature optimally. In order to carry out the sealing process successfully, the wine should be bottled in dark bottles to protect it from light, which can affect the quality of the wine. Before inserting the cork, it is important to ensure that there is about two finger widths of air between the liquid and the cork. This space allows the wine to expand if necessary without pushing the cork out of the bottle. Once the bottles have been corked, cork hoods or champagne knots should be used to secure the cork and prevent air or foreign matter from entering. The bottles are then placed in a water bath and heated at a constant temperature of 65 °C for around 20 minutes. This process serves to kill any germs and microorganisms that may be present and to ensure that the cork is optimally sealed. After heating, the cork hoods or champagne knots are removed and the bottles are stored horizontally. This ensures that the cork remains moist, which is an important prerequisite for a good seal and helps the wine to retain its quality and ageing potential over a longer period of time.

Screw cap

Similar to with the use of corks, the wine should be bottled in dark bottles to protect it from light. There should also be about two fingers' width of air between the liquid and the top of the bottle. The bottles are then placed open in a water bath and heated at a constant temperature of 65 °C for around 20 minutes. This process also serves to kill any germs and micro-organisms that may be present and to ensure that the screw cap seals well. After heating, the cap is placed on the bottle, and the bottles are slowly cooled. This creates a vacuum that holds the screw cap securely on the bottle.

17. Step-by-step guide to the individual stages of wine-making

Step 1: Before you start making wine, you should obtain the necessary equipment.

Step 2: Prepare the fermentation starter two to three days before you start making wine.

Step 3: Choose the fruit you want to use for the wine carefully. Make sure it is ripe and of good quality. Wash the fruit thoroughly and remove any rotten fruit or damaged areas. These could otherwise affect the flavour and quality of the wine. Also remove the seeds and stones from the fruit so that only the flesh remains.

Step 4: Depending on the type of wine you want to make, now make the mash or the juice.

Step 5: Calculate the amount of sugar and water required for the wine. Dissolve only one third of the calculated amount of sugar in water and add it to the sulphurised fermentation vessel together with the mash or juice. Make sure that the vessel is only two-thirds full to leave enough space for the fermentation process.

Note: The remaining two thirds of sugar is added at a later stage. If the sugar is added all at once, there is a risk that the fermentation process could get out of hand and the yeast would then be weakened by the resulting heat. There is a risk of stuck fermentation.

Step 6: Fill the fermentation vessel with the mash or juice and attach the fermentation tube with stopper. The fermentation tube enables the exchange of gases during fermentation and prevents air from entering the vessel. Now carefully transport the vessel into the fermentation chamber.

Step 7: After three to four days, the second addition of sugar takes place. Again, one third of the calculated total amount of sugar is dissolved in a little water and added to the wine mixture. The fermentation tube with stopper is reattached.

Step 8: After a further eight days, the third addition of sugar takes place, as already described in step 7. This process supports fermentation and helps to achieve the desired alcohol content in the wine (the last third of the calculated total amount of sugar is added).

Step 9: Approximately two to three weeks after the last addition of sugar, there should no longer be any noticeable fermentation in the fermentation tube. Now it is time for the first racking. This involves drawing the wine off from the settled yeast and turbidity and decanting it into a new, full container.

This procedure promotes the clarity of the wine and prepares it for further storage.

Note: The new container must be filled to the brim. If this is not possible, glass balls (marbles) are used to help, which are gradually submerged in the vessel. This is repeated until the vessel is filled to the brim, and then the wine must is placed in the cellar and left there for three to four weeks.

Step 10: After the first racking, you can decide whether you want to carry out a second racking. The same procedure as in step 9 is used (from the second sentence).

Step 11: Now it's time to taste the wine and decide whether you want a bitter or sweet wine. For a sweet wine, add about 40 to 60 g of sugar per 1 litre of wine. The sugar/water ratio is four parts sugar to one part water. Adjust the flavour of the wine carefully and add the sugar cautiously.

Step 12: Now you can fill the wine into the bottles, depending on which closure you have chosen. You have the option of pasteurising the wine before sealing. This extends the shelf life of the wine and prevents re-fermentation in the bottle.

Step 13: Take the filled wine bottles to the storage room or cellar. The bottles should be left there for three to four weeks so that the wine can continue to develop and mature.

Step 14: After storage, the wine is now ready to enjoy. You can attach labels with the name and vintage of the wine in order to label it properly.

Step 15: Enjoy your homemade wine with friends and family. Try different varieties and be surprised by the different aromas and flavours.

<u>Note</u>: If you are aiming for maximum precision in winemaking, I recommend that you retain a small portion of the total calculated amount of water to be added. This trick allows you to dissolve the individual sugar additions for the wine in the remaining water. Why is this important? By doing this, you avoid possibly overstretching the wine and thus reduce the risk of wine diseases. Overstretching can occur if too much water is added. This lowers the acidity in the wine and makes it more susceptible to wine diseases.

18. Multi-fruit wines

The multi-fruit winemaking technique is particularly suitable for advanced winemakers who want to expand their winemaking skills and create a variety of flavours. This technique can even be used with fruits that are not normally well suited to winemaking. Let's take pear wine as an example. Due to its low acidity, it is not ideal for winemaking, as it would normally lack the refreshing and tangy flavour. There is also an increased risk of wine diseases. However, a solution can be found with a creative approach. By mixing pear juice with rhubarb juice, for example, a tasty pear and rhubarb wine can be produced. It is important to calculate the required quantities of water and sugar in the fruit and scale them to the desired volume of wine to be produced.

Some fruits have different harvest times, so it may be necessary to pasteurise the fruits that are harvested first in order to preserve them before they can be fermented together with the other fruits. It is important that the juices are always fermented together in order to achieve a homogeneous development of flavour.

Here are some examples of tasty multi-fruit wines:

- Currant & gooseberry
- Apple, gooseberry & rhubarb
- Raspberry, sour cherry & redcurrant
- Sour cherry, blueberry & redcurrant

Tip: Cider is particularly recommended for beginners as it already has an acidity of 8 g/litre and no additional water needs to be added. As a result, there is no risk of overstretching and susceptibility to wine diseases.

The multi-fruit winemaking method allows wine lovers to express their creativity and create unique wine variations that are both flavourful and aesthetically pleasing. It is a way to combine different fruits and create harmonious wines with complex flavours that delight the senses.

19. Wine diseases

Vinegar taint

Vinegar taint is one of the most common and unpleasant wine diseases. It manifests itself through a distinct vinegar odour and a vinegary taste in the wine. In advanced cases, a slimy secretion, known as mother of vinegar, may appear on the surface. Vinegar taint is caused by sloppy work, rotten fruit that has stood too long, or air ingress during mashing or fermentation. High alcohol and acid content in the wine create unfavourable conditions for microorganisms, which prevents their development. In order to avoid vinegar taint, clean and fast work as well as an airtight seal and rapid fermentation are crucial. Unfortunately, there is no way to return the wine to its original state. The wine is considered spoilt and can only be processed into vinegar

Mannitol fermentation

Mannitol fermentation is another undesirable wine disease that is characterised by a peculiar taste and causes a scratchy sensation in the throat, similar to a slight vinegar taste. This change occurs because the wine has insufficient acidity, is stored too warm or is racked too late. To avoid mannitol fermentation, the wine should not be overstretched, should not be stored too warm and should be racked in good time. As a measure, it is recommended that the fermentation vessel is racked several times and sulphurised in the process.

This process aims to eliminate the problem and reduce undesirable changes in flavour. However, it is important to note that it may not be possible to eliminate the problem entirely. Nevertheless, repeated racking and sulphurisation of the fermentation vessel can improve the situation and protect the quality of the wine.

Lactic acid taint

Lactic acid taint leads to a flavour and taste in the wine that is reminiscent of sauerkraut or pickled gherkin brine. This wine disease is caused by too little acidity, which leads to a disproportionate conversion of sugar into lactic acid. To avoid this, care should be taken not to overstretch the wine and not to store it too warm. Timely decanting is also important. Although an unpleasant flavour is already present, progression of the problem can be halted by re-racking and sulphurisation. These measures serve to stabilise the situation and prevent further negative developments.

Surface film

Surface film is a change on the surface of the wine and manifests itself as a greyish-white, greyish or reddish-grey skin. This change occurs when fermentation stalls, the wine is fermented or stored too warm and the acidity is too low. To avoid surface film, the wine should be fermented sufficiently and stored at a moderate temperature. After racking, the wine can be stored in the cellar.

To prevent air from entering and thus the spread of surface film, the fermentation vessel should be filled to the brim. If surface film is already present, fresh racking and sulphurisation can help to stop its progression. Unfortunately, the unpleasant flavour often persists in such cases.

Ropiness

Ropiness is characterised by a thick, slimy wine that is stringy when poured. This phenomenon occurs when the acidity of the wine is too low. To avoid ropiness, the wine should not be over-fermented, rapid fermentation at appropriate temperatures should be ensured and the wine should be racked in good time. If ropiness has already occurred, you can try pouring the wine into another container and breaking up the slime, followed by sulphurisation.

Butyric acid taint

Butyric acid taint is characterised by a smell of rancid butter in the wine. This also occurs because the acidity in the wine is too low. To avoid butyric acid taint, the wine should not be overstretched. Once butyric acid taint has occurred, it is difficult to eliminate, and there is no possibility of further processing the wine into vinegar. In such cases, the only option is to dispose of the wine.

20. Wine flaws

Blue casse

Blue casse is characterised by a blackish discolouration of the wine, which occurs when it comes into contact with iron and combines with the tannins in the wine. To avoid blue casse, the wine should not come into contact with iron. If this discolouration occurs, it can be partially remedied by blue fining or adding lemon juice. In the case of blue fining, potassium ferrocyanide (yellow prussiate of potash, $K_4[Fe(CN)_6]$) is used to restore the colour.

White casse

White casse, on the other hand, is characterised by a whitish or greyish turbidity in the wine, which is also due to a reaction with iron. Here too, the wine should be prevented from coming into contact with iron. A similar measure to that used in the event of blue casse, i.e. blue fining with potassium ferrocyanide or the addition of lemon juice, can help to partially restore the colour of the wine.

Off-odour caused by excess sulphur

An excess sulphur-induced off-odour occurs when some of the sulphur does not drain off completely during sulphurisation of the fermentation vessel and remains in the vessel. In order to avoid an excess sulphur-induced off-odour, it is important to remove the sulphur completely. If this unpleasant odour still occurs in the wine, it can be eliminated by decanting into a lightly-sulphurised fermentation vessel.

Yeast-induced off-odour

A yeast-induced off-odour, on the other hand, occurs if the wine is left on the yeast in a warm room for too long after fermentation. This causes the yeast component, which produces hydrogen sulphide, to develop an unpleasant rotten egg odour. In order to avoid a yeast-induced off-odour, it is advisable to rack the wine immediately after fermentation has finished. Decanting into a lightly-sulphurised fermentation vessel can also minimise possible odour problems.

21. Vinegar preparation

If the wine does not turn out as planned and has unpleasant flavours or odours, there is indeed the option of making wine vinegar from it instead of throwing it away immediately. Here are the steps to make wine vinegar from a failed wine:

Step 1: Choose a suitable vinegar fermentation vessel. Ideally, it should have a large surface area to maximise the formation of vinegar bacteria. Vinegar fermentation vessels made of wood, clay or stainless steel are well suited.

Step 2: Heat the wine to 32 °C and then pour it into the vinegar fermentation vessel. Add some nutrient salt (e. g. ammonium chloride) and 10 percent household vinegar to the wine to promote the formation of acetic acid bacteria.

Step 3: Protect the vinegar fermentation vessel from vinegar flies with fine gauze or muslin, and leave it at a temperature of 20 °C to 25 °C for three to four weeks. During this time, the acetic acid bacteria convert the alcohol in the wine into vinegar.

Step 4: After three to four weeks, carry out a taste test to check whether the wine has already turned to vinegar. If the vinegar is not yet acidic enough, the fermentation time must be extended. As soon as the vinegar has reached the desired flavour, the wine can be strained through a cloth to separate it from the slimy mother of vinegar.

Making wine vinegar is a way of not completely wasting an unsuccessful wine and instead obtaining a new product. However, it is important to remember that the conversion to wine vinegar takes time and patience, and the result may not be exactly the same as traditional wine vinegar. Nevertheless, it can be a worthwhile option to turn a failed wine into a usable vinegar.

22. Summary

Winemaking is a fascinating and demanding art that can be a rewarding experience for both beginners and experienced amateur winemakers. In order for the wine to be successful and its quality guaranteed, a few important steps and requirements must be observed.

Clean and fast processing of the fruits

It is crucial that the fruit used is clean and ripe. Rotten or spoilt fruit should be discarded without fail, as this can spoil the wine. In addition, the fruit should be processed as soon as possible after harvest or purchase to ensure optimum condition and flavour.

Light and oxygen protection

Light and oxygen can oxidise the wine and cause undesirable changes in taste. It is therefore important to protect the wine from direct sunlight and contact with oxygen during fermentation and storage. Dark bottles and well-sealed containers are helpful here.

Moderate use of sulphur

Sulphur is used as a preservative in winemaking as it prevents the growth of undesirable microorganisms. However, the use of sulphur should be kept as low as possible, as too much sulphur can affect the flavour of the wine. Excessive use of sulphur can also lead to allergic reactions.

Preparation and meticulousness

Before you start making wine, it is advisable to prepare each step of the process carefully. Make sure you have the necessary equipment and ingredients ready. The exact dosage and adherence to the individual steps are decisive for the success of the wine. Stick to the recommended times and temperatures to achieve optimum results.

Recommendation for beginners: Cider

An apple wine, also known as cider, is recommended for beginners. Apples generally have an appropriate acidity level, which reduces the risk of wine diseases. Cider is comparatively easy to make and offers scope for experimentation and variation. It is a refreshing and popular drink that is enjoyed by many wine lovers.

Winemaking requires patience, dedication and willingness to experiment. With the right approach and knowledge of the individual steps, you can make delicious wines from different fruits and create your own personalised wine experience. It is important to gain experience in order to perfect your own wine production and discover the variety of aromas and flavours that the world of wine has to offer.

Now that you have acquired this comprehensive knowledge, you will be able to create your very own excellent wine. May the art of winemaking give you much pleasure and be crowned with success. I encourage you to use your newly-acquired expertise with enthusiasm and to create incomparable wines. Cheers to your masterpiece of winemaking – a feast for the senses and a delight for every palate. Cheers to your future wine creations and the unforgettable moments that may accompany them.

ABOUT THE AUTHOR

As a graduate of automotive technology and a qualified engineer, I have successfully used my professional expertise in product development at a renowned automotive supplier. In addition to my professional career, I discovered my passion for winemaking and devoted myself to this fascinating hobby. I have acquired extensive knowledge in the field of winemaking, which I have combined with meticulous research and additional professional sources in this book.

It is my ambition to take readers on an informative and challenging journey into the world of winemaking. I hope that this book not only provides valuable insights for beginners, but also inspires and enriches experienced wine lovers.

May this book be a useful companion to inspire your own winemaking and give you joy and enjoyment in every bottle.

Cheers! 🍷

Impressum

Dipl. -Ing. (FH) Tobias Gehring

Fröbelstraße 2

08209 Auerbach

list of references

Brett Jordan (22.07.2019): Presskorken, [online] https://uns-plash.com/photos/W2i3-Ra2Ls4, [abgerufen am: 03.10.2022 13:03Uhr]

Liza Tkachuk (11.09.2021): Synthetischer Korken, [online] iStock Lizenz-1339671609, [abgerufen am: 06.10.2022]

Figure 14: Adobe Stock_480375570

Weinfreunde (18.10.2016): Korken, Glasstopfen & Co., [on-line] https://www.weinfreunde.de/magazin/weinwissen/kor-ken-schraubverschluss-co-viel-diskutiert-und-zu-wenig-be-dacht/, [abgerufen am: 31.01.2022 19:16Uhr]

Advanco GmbH (04.08.2022): Weinhefen: Übersicht der Rein-zuchthefe-Sorten und Preise, [online] https://www.hausgar-ten.net/garten-kreativ/weinherstellung/weinhefe-wo-kau-fen.html, [abgerufen am: 08.09.2022 21:16Uhr]

Mercateo Deutschland AG (keine Angabe): Weinhefe, [on-line] https://www.mercateo.com/p/400-1810142/Wein-hefe_fuer_50l_Zeltinger.html?ViewName=live&swit-chToCountry=DE&switchToLanguage=de&chooseGeo=true, [abgerufen am: 01.02.2022 21:17Uhr]

Dr. Andreas Kranz (13.03.2021): 9. Die Hefe [online] https://fruchtweinkeller.de/anleitungen/fruchtweine/9-die-hefe/, [abgerufen am: 03.02.2022 21:12Uhr]

https://xtools.wmflabs.org/articleinfo-authorship/de.wikipe-dia.org/Kahmhaut?uselang=de (26.10.2021): Kahmhaut [on-line] https://de.wikipedia.org/wiki/Kahmhaut, [abgerufen am: 03.02.2022 19:19Uhr]

Obstwein selbst gemacht, Professor Ehrhard Donath, sechs-zigste Auflage 1971, VEB Fachbuchverlag Leipzig

Alexander Ultes (10.05.2016): Glycerin [online] https://wein-fachberater.der-ultes.de/enzyklopaedie/glycerin/, [abgerufen am: 06.02.2022 10:19Uhr]

Gastro Brennecke GmbH & Co. KG (keine Angabe): Kitzinger Weinhefe & Co., [online] https://gastro-brennecke.de/wein-saft/weinhefe/?p=2, [abgerufen am: 06.02.2022 11:10Uhr]

wein.plus (18.08.2022): Hefenährsalz, [online] https://glossar.wein.plus/hefenaehrsalze, [abgerufen am: 26.08.2022 12:00Uhr]

das deutsche weinmagazin (22.08.2009): Welche Nahrung braucht die Hefe?, [online] https://www.wbi-bw.de/pb/site/pbs-bw-new/get/documents/MLR.LEL/PB5Documents/wbi/011%20Fachartikel/0115%20FA%20Referat%2021%20Oenolo-gie%20und%20Versuchskelle-rei/1151_09%20FA%202009%20und%20%C3%A4lter_Vortr%C3%A4ge%20Brosch%C3%BCren%20Faltbl%C3%A4tter/Welche-Nahrung-braucht-die%20Hefe%20DDW%202009.pdf?attach-ment=true [abgerufen am: 06.02.2022 21:00Uhr]

wein.plus (18.08.2022): Hefenährsalz, [online] https://glossar.wein.plus/hefenaehrsalze, [abgerufen am: 29.08.2022 19:03Uhr]

wein.plus (11.12.2021): Heferinde, [online] https://glossar.wein.plus/heferinde, [abgerufen am:07.02.2022 19:06Uhr]

Schliessmann Schwäbisch Hall (11/20212), Hefezellwand, [online] https://www.google.com/url?sa=t&rct=j&q=&esrc=s&source=web&cd=&cad=rja&uact=8&ved=2ahUKEwiU1N_Yiu71A-hURSfEDHSnwCMoQFnoECAgQAQ&url=https%3A%2F%2Fc-schliessmann.de%2Fmedia%2Fhefezell-wand.pdf&usg=AOvVaw2zL_Mtk1m3kcysKzeH3f4q, [abgerufen am: 07.02.2022 19:09Uhr]

Eaton (05/2017): Hefenährstoffe und Weineschönungsprodukte auf Hefebasis Navigator, [online] https://docplayer.org/51262508-Beverage-treatment-products-hefenaehrstoffe-und-Weineschoenungsprodukte-auf-hefebasis-navigator.html [abgerufen am: 07.02.2022 19:16Uhr]

Studyflix GmbH (keine Angabe): Lysozym, [online] https://studyflix.de/biologie/lysozym-3105, [abgerufen am: 07.02.2022 19:19Uhr]

vitipendium (19.02.2014): Verwendung von Hefenährstoffen, [online] http://www.vitipendium.de/Verwendung_von_Hefen%C3%A4hrstoffen, [abgerufen am: 08.02.2022 19:33Uhr]

Studyflix GmbH (keine Angabe): Adsorbtion [online] https://studyflix.de/chemie/adsorption-1773, [abgerufen am: 08.02.2022 19:50Uhr

Ing. Wolfgang Renner (keine Angabe): Aktivierung der Hefen! [online] https://www.google.com/url?sa=t&rct=j&q=&esrc=s&source=web&cd=&cad=rja&uact=8&ved=2ahUKEwjQzu-Wmn_P1AhWN-aQKHUVhAn-MQFnoECDUQAQ&url=https%3A%2F%2Fwww.agrar.steiermark.at%2Fcms%2Fdokumente%2F10936035_11731059%2F7ad5dc6f%2F2004%2520Winzer-Hefeaktivit%25C3%25A4t.pdf&usg=AOvVaw1ZcgFG62ZO6S9I6UIEWsqW, [abgerufen am: 09.02.2022 21:22Uhr]

Prof. Dr. Doris Rauheit (keine Angabe): Zusatz von Hefenährstoffen zu Traubenmosten, [online] https://www.google.com/url?sa=t&rct=j&q=&esrc=s&source=web&cd=&ved=2ahUKEwjetNeBqPP1AhXSPOw-KHd9wBDMQFnoECAUQAw&url=https%3A%2F%2Fservice.ble.de%2Fptdb%2Findex2.php%3Fdetail_id%3D99954%26site_key%3D145%26zeilenzahl_zaehler%3D590%26NextRow%3D580%26pld%3D99954%26dld%3D114927&usg=AOvVaw33cYl2V9FKvAZGTazf_u_n, [abgerufen am: 09.02.2022 21:40Uhr]

das deutsche weinmagazin (09.11.2013): Haltbarkeit von Weißwein, [online] https://silo.tips/download/haltbarkeit-von-weiwein, [abgerufen am: 10.02.2022 10:15Uhr]

Bundesinstitut für Risikobewertung (18.01.2019): Was sind Sterine?, [online] https://www.bfr.bund.de/cd/9504, [abgerufen am: 10.02.2022 11:10Uhr]

IOC: (28.06.2018): ACTIVIT, [online] https://ioc.eu.com/de/produktdatenblaetter/aktivatoren-der-alkoholischen-garung/, [abgerufen am: 10.02.2022 18:00Uhr]

Eaton (11/2019): Hefenährstoff SIHA PROFERM Arom+ [online] https://www.eaton.com/de/de-de/catalog/yeast-nutrients/siha-proferm-arom.resources.html, [abgerufen am: 14.02.2022 19:13Uhr]

Wein hausgemacht, Eigener Wein aus Trauben, Obst, Kräutern und Blüten, Herbert Feldkamp, Verlag: Ludwig

Figure 10: Refractometer , AdobeStock_399612246 [online], [abgerufen am: 03.10.2022 19:08]

Figure 11: Acidometer, AdobeStock_435278259 [online], [abgerufen am: 03.10.2022 20:09]

Step Systems GmbH (2019): Refraktometer, [online] https://shop.stepsystems.de/images/BDA/25010_Refrakto-meter.pdf, [abgerufen am: 02.04.2022 13:30Uhr]

Königin Luisen Gymnasium Erfurt (keine Angabe): Station 1: Herstellung von Essig, [online] https://www.google.com/url?sa=t&rct=j&q=&esrc=s&source=web&cd=&cad=rja&uact=8&ved=2ahU-KEwiF5_nntpb2AhXpSfEDHRkNAQ4QFnoE-CAMQAQ&url=http%3A%2F%2Fwww.klg-erfurt.de%2Ffi-les%2F0%2F1%2F0%2F3983.pdf&usg=AOvVaw0mrHI-zyp_K8ywm3x4EycJ_ , [abgerufen am: 23.02.2022 19:10Uhr]

wein.plus (23.06.2021): Autolyse [online] https://glossar.wein.plus/autolyse, [abgerufen am: 15.02.2022 19:20Uhr]

Dr. Andreas Kranz (13.03.2021): 9. Die Hefe, [online] https://fruchtweinkeller.de/anleitungen/fruchtweine/9-die-hefe/, [abgerufen am: 07.02.2022 19:09Uhr]

vitipendium (17.02.2014): Blauschönung, [online] http://www.vitipendium.de/Blausch%C3%B6nung, [abgeru-fen am: 19.02.2022 12:16Uhr]

Figure 6: Gärstarter: AdobeStock_172128085 [online], [abge-rufen am: 03.10.2022]

Kitzinger Reinzuchthefe (keine Angabe): Gebrauchsanwei-sung für Meßinstrumente, [online] https://www.google.com/url?sa=t&rct=j&q=&esrc=s&source=web&cd=&cad=rja&uact=8&ved=2ahU-KEwiJ3Pj7uoL3AhXagP0HHUeKDX0QFnoE-CAgQAw&url=https%3A%2F%2Fwww.hobbybrauerver-sand.de%2Fmediafiles%2FAnleitungen%2FArauner%2FAcido-meter_Vinome-ter_DINA5_web.pdf&usg=AOvVaw0jp9STwYXMK8CHI-RcA0QZM, [abgerufen am: 07.04.2022 19:03Uhr]

Arauner Kitzingen (keine Angabe): Acidometer Glaszylinder 20 ml mit Fuß und Ring [online] https://www.arauner.com/messintrumente-zubehoer/342/acidometer-glaszylinder-20-ml-mit-fuss-undbr/ring?c=9000006, [abgerufen am: 07.04.2022 19:09Uhr]

Marianne und Wilfried Marquardt (keine Angabe): Bentonitschönung [online] http://www.hobbymosterei.de/html/bentonitschoenung.html, [abgerufen am: 18.04.2022 12:00Uhr]

Vitipendium (06.02.2014): Bentonitschönung [online] http://www.vitipendium.de/Bentoniteinsatz, [abgerufen am: 18.04.2022 12:30Uhr]

Figure 4: , AdobeStock_412853215 [online], [abgerufen am: 03.10.2022 13:00Uhr]

Figure 2: , AdobeStock_44292774 [online], [abgerufen am: 03.10.2022 13:01]

Figure 3: , AdobeStock_55011416 [online], [abgerufen am: 03.10.2022 13:33

Figure 1: [online] https://pixabay.com/de/photos/ballon-weinballon-ballonflasche-2515660/, [abgerufen am: 03.10.2022 13:20Uhr]

Printed in Dunstable, United Kingdom

65264009R00067